Nailed It!
(Wisdom For New Nail Technicians)

Copyright @2020 By Angeline Belus-Andre

Nailed It!
(Wisdom For New Nail Technicians)

All rights reserved. This book or any portion thereof may not be reproduced or used in any manner whatsoever without the express written permission of the publisher except for the use of brief quotations in a book review.

Published in The United States of America

Cover Design
Kingdom Impressions Ink, LLC
design.kiink@gmail.com

Book Development & Editing
Coach B Write For Me LLC
CoachB@HelpMeCoachB.Org
www.HelpMeCoachB.Org

Author's Contact Information
Favor Nails LLC
favornailsbyangie@gmail.com
favornails.org

Table Of Contents

Wisdom #1   22
(Connect With Your Passion)
- Identifying What Inspired You
- Embracing What You Love About It
- Opening Your Heart

Wisdom #2   28
(No Pain, No Gain)
- Creating A Strategy
- Researching Marketing Strategies
- Becoming An Original

Wisdom #3   34
(Money Decisions)
- Recognizing Priority Over Unnecessary
- Building Your Inventory
- Create A Budget

Wisdom #4   40
(Encourage Yourself)
- Utilizing Your Circle For Assistance
- Enduring Slow Seasons
- Believing In Your Brand

Wisdom #5   46
(Prepare For Turbulence)
- Setting Healthy Boundaries
- Researching Credibility
- Allowing Experience To Teach You

Wisdom #6   52
(Submit To Assistance)
- Humbling Yourself & Remain Teachable
- Taking Notes & Asking Questions
- Choosing Your Mentors Wisely

Wisdom #7   58
(Break Bad Habits)
- The Results Of Bad Habits
- Identifying Bad Habits & Triggers
- Maintaining Professionalism

Wisdom #8   63
(Be Strategic)
- Rejecting Anxiousness
- Choosing The Right Location
- Marketing Matters

Wisdom #9   68
(Scheduling Matters)
- Effective Booking
- Keeping Back-up Scheduling Book
- Avoiding Overbooking

Wisdom #10   73
(Refresh Your Clients)
- Setting A Caring Atmosphere
- Serving More Than Nail Care
- Providing What They Won't

Wisdom #11   78
(Cancellations & Rescheduling)
- Establishing Order
- Cancellation Fees
- Client Respect & Business Standards

Wisdom #12   83
(You Are What You Wear)
- Avoiding Discomfort
- Maintaining Fashion & Professionalism
- Business Attire & Choices

"Author's Biography"

Mrs. Angeline Belus-Andre, CEO of Favor Nails LLC, is a beautiful wife and mother residing in the South Florida area. She has served her current region as a licensed nail technician for over a decade and is taking the nail industry by force.

She was born in Freeport Bahamas, where her Caribbean life experience gave her endless inspiration. It helped initiate her sharp eye for color, textures, and also shapes.

Mrs. Belus-Andre both attended and graduated from Margate Beauty School, and she immediately began to seek professional development by taking classes with some of the world's best nail techs. She firmly believes that if you want to be the best, you have to train with the best.

In return for putting in hard work and discipline, Angeline has worked with CEOs, pastors, celebrities, influential women, and her favorite, everyday women. She made a vow to always breathe excitement into people's lives by beautifying their nails.

She is active in her local community and has been awarded as a community activist amongst many other great women. She is a new author and has recently released her new oil, "Favorable Oil," that is beneficial for hair, nails, and skin.

She attends a local church weekly where she is building her faith and is being equipped spiritually to remain committed to her purpose. She is currently networking and preparing to expand her business as a nail tech to breathe more excitement all over the world.

She loves educating and inspiring nail technicians. She has a heart for those who desire to go further in their career and become successful.

Her ultimate goal is to bring professionalism, creativity, and growth into the nail industry. She desires to see every nail technician, "Nail It!!"

Foreword

The time that we spend in the presence of one another is precious, to say the least. When do we seriously take that time to reflect on what we have to share and what was shared with us during the exchange of time?

In this era, many are distracted by the many tools and gadgets that have given us live access to the lives of millions of people worldwide. As you turn the pages of this book, I want you to reflect on the importance of "being present."

Living for the precious moments you have with everyone you encounter. Wisdom is the principal thing, and it's hidden in the innermost parts of those around us.

Think back to a time when you may have sat down with an older person to chat, were you enlightened? Many lessons, examples, support, and comfort as well can be found in the moments that we have forgotten how to live in with one another.

Elders have always been the keepers of wisdom; however, it's a known fact that through experience in different areas, it can be gained at any age. I charge you that will read the pages of this book to live in the experiences that you will find in the pages and garner the wisdom that is imparted here.

The more wisdom you gain, the greater the living you will obtain. It is a known fact that the richest man that ever lived prayed for a single gift from God; that gift was wisdom.

In order to have it, you must seek it, and in order to find it, you must search. After you read this book, you will never see your time at the table with someone the same.

If it is nails, hair, coffee, or casual chats, you will see here that in every moment there is something to be shared. Take time away from the idleness of distractions and talk to the person servicing you; your words could lead to an enlightened path, a healed hurt, or the change of a course totally.

You will never know if you don't spend some time sharing with each other. I believe that this book will not only teach from the perspective of practical skill, but that it will also bring to light the importance of verbal communication, eye contact, body language, and physical touch.

Angeline has put the time into her craft and skill. It shows in her care for her clients.

This is her heart's work to not only serve her clients, but to serve her peers by imparting wisdom through skill and experience. Having the desire to serve people in any capacity is a gift within itself; knowing how to serve is the real blessing.

This book will teach you how to be the blessing.

-Dr. Rasheda Jackson

Introduction

Favor Nails is my baby! It is the business that I gave birth to and has nurtured and developed with love, strategy, and commitment. It is my motivation, investment, and the reason that I have met so many amazing people in my life. Favor Nails has allowed me to serve in many local communities, including house calls to well-known individuals. This business was only a dream when I started school to become a nail technician, but I knew that one day, it would be my very reality.

I worked very hard to build Favor Nails, and even now, I have made a vow always to give it 100%. I love what I do as a nail technician, and I love how I do it. I have confidence in my brand, and I have faith in you. I wrote this book to help inspire, encourage, and enlighten you as a new nail technician. I wish this book were available for me when I first graduated and launched my nail business.

However, I'm grateful for my experience and this opportunity to pour into you. This industry can be exciting and hard at the same time, but it is how you choose to perceive and prepare for it. This book is to help you adjust your perception and to prepare you for the ups and downs that you will experience on this journey. You have the potential to be the best nail technician in your local community, city, and state, and I want to help you embrace this.

There are many things that you may have learned in the nail academy, but there are so many other things that you will only learn along the way.

This book includes wisdom and advice on finding the right location, building clientele, maintaining professionalism, connecting with mentors, and allowing your creativity to run wild without limits and boundaries. I don't have the answer to every question that you may have, but I have intentionally addressed areas that I've had the most issues with or have witnessed other nail techs experience. We all have different paths and roads to take in our lives, but principles don't change. Apply everything that you will read and make a vow to live by it. There's a quote that says, "We only learn by experience," but I beg to differ.

There are many things that we can avoid if we would open up our hearts and minds to receive advice and wisdom from someone who has traveled the path that we are preparing to take. I encourage you now to use every passage in this book to help you avoid running into a brick wall. Please use this impartation when you have questions and no one to answer them, and in your spare time, allow it to live inside of your heart. The more you learn, the more you will be prepared to endure the test and challenges that will come before you. Always increase your knowledge as much as you can outside of this book as well.

If you are a former nail tech that gave up or is lacking stability, this book is for you too. The power is in your hands to become successful! To become unstoppable! To become limitless! You hold power to "Nail It"!

"Breathing Excitement Into Your Life."

#1
"Connect With Your Passion"

I have always loved caring for people. While growing up, this passion could have led me to the nursing field, but God had other plans for my life. He has a way of using our gifts and passions to not only be used in the church, but God will also allow our gifts to flow in the marketplace. As I grew older, I became more aware of my creativity and my eye for shapes, designs, and colors. It made me light up to see a new polish in the store, a new design on someone's nails, or a material.

I knew within myself that if someone could experience the creativity that was going on in my head, they would feel this same excitement. When I begin to embrace the nail tech life, I immediately created my slogan, "Breathing Excitement Into Your Life."

Footnote: "Passion will take your business to the next level."

I knew that this was one of my gifts and became more and more inspired after each client. Designing, nurturing, and creating beauty on the hands and feet of others gave me a joy that I can't explain, even when I was only testing it out to see if it was really for me. I met so many people as a beginner, and I realized that my chair was not just a place to sit for nail care, but it was also a place to relax for spiritual and emotional care.

The more smiles I put on a client's face, the more I was inspired to learn more and become a better nail technician. To be an effective nail technician, you must first be inspired. Something in you has to spark when you think of it, do it, or even decide to practice it.

Footnote: "Passion is a fuel, use it to go after your purpose."

I have been in the nail industry for over a decade now, and it has been an inspiration that has kept me faithful and committed to growing. You will encounter many challenges in your career and your personal life as well, but never allow the pain nor chaos of it to shut down your passion.

When your passion dies, so will your creativity and clientele. As a new nail tech, passion has to be pursued daily to avoid stagnation and distractions. It will keep you connected to your craft and your clients. Every person that you will serve will have the ability to feel your passion, so be sure to be as passionate as you can when they arrive. No one desires to pay a tech their hard-earned money if the tech does not care how their work comes out.

Footnote: "Passion is necessary for success."

A client that feels and sees your passion is one who will not want to work with anyone else. You have the power to build a consistent clientele through the power of your creativity. Never take your creativity for granted. Utilize it to build your legacy. Connect with more than your creativity, connect with your passion!

Footnote: "The lack of passion could be the cause of the lack of success."

"You gain strength, courage, and confidence by every experience in which you really stop to look fear in the face. You are able to say to yourself, 'I lived through this horror. I can take the next thing that comes along."
-**Eleanor Roosevelt**

#2
"No Pain, No Gain"

Being a nail tech sounds very simple to many, but it is not a position to treat as a hobby. There are standards that you must keep and guidelines that you must follow. Becoming a nail technician must begin with education and training, so there is no going around the challenge of having to enroll in a class, pay school fees, and apply for your license to perform professional services. On top of this, you must also deal with competitors, client's inconsistency, keeping your inventory stocked, and finding a great location to run your business. I have experienced other techs stealing and advertising my designs, drama working in toxic shops, and there were times when I didn't have a place to run my business and still had to keep my passion and zeal.

Footnote: "*Gaining anything in life requires pain in some capacity.*"

There are thousands of nail techs in this world, so you must have courage, confidence, and tenacity to keep going even when you have little to no clients. There will be high and low seasons in this industry, but when you are in the low seasons, this is not the time to feel defeated, but to work harder and to increase your knowledge on new designs, polish types, colors, etc. You may have to work a regular job and work as a nail tech in some seasons but endure no matter how hard it may seem. No matter how talented you are, or how low your prices are, in the beginning, clients will not immediately run you down. This could cause you to give up quickly or attempt to be like someone else in hopes of getting clients.

Footnote: "Working hard must become a lifestyle."

This is very dangerous, please avoid the copycat spirit and stay true to your vision for your business, designs, and aim to be an original. This journey can be rough if you do not believe in yourself and is not willing to work hard, no matter how many clients you have. Always remember that your low seasons are not the end of your story unless you allow it to be. Embrace the challenges of being a new nail technician as learning and growing moments. If you learn from the difficulties and the potential hardship, it may cause you never to experience them again.

Be open to making mistakes, but never allow yourself to become comfortable with not fixing them. Work harder than expected, longer than you desire, and more than you make plans to.

Footnote: *"Give your business your all."*

In the beginning, practice and marketing must become the new air that you breathe. It may be the only thing you need to do in your spare time. Become one with stretching yourself past your comfort zone.

Footnote: "If there's no pain, there will probably be no gain."

"Invest in yourself. Your career is the engine of your wealth."
-Paul Clitheroe

#3
"Money Decisions"

I started my business from the ground up, and it took more than creativity to run it. It required finances and many sacrifices as well. As a new nail technician, you will have to purchase your supplies and equipment to make sure that they run professionally and to build a healthy clientele. You will have to make wise decisions with your income, and sacrifice will be a road that you will have to travel. Your old spending habits must be stopped and revised to make sure that you have all the necessities needed.

I sacrificed a lot to purchase the needs of my business, but I knew it was all worth it. Sometimes, you will be forced to choose between buying what you want and what you need, determine what you need.

Footnote: "Spend wisely but make it worth the sacrifice."

Before you can make any money, you will have to spend money. It is a part of the building process. It is very healthy to create a business plan and a budget each month to help you remain committed to purchasing things for your business.

On top of buying supplies, you will also have a shop or rental fee. Money may become very tight, but if you commit to spending wisely and strategizing priorities from things that can hold off a little, you will survive. You must also decide to purchase equipment and supplies that have quality. Buying cheap items will only keep you buying things over and over when things continue to break or be of no practical use. As you make money, please also learn how to save money.

Footnote: "Be creative; receive compensation in more ways than one."

Your clients will always look forward to quality equipment, polish, etc., make sure that they experience it. Try very hard to maintain good spending habits and making sure priority products are purchased and available. As a new tech, never be afraid to have a donation box on your desk. It is perfectly ok to allow your clients and others to donate and give into your vision for the new business. I also recommend creating and selling other products that your clients will need or uses on a daily basis.

If you need help managing your finances for your new business, seek out a financial coach or classes to help you adjust. Do not try to manage on your own. Receiving assistance will help you get to the next level effectively without regrets.

Footnote: *"Always invest in yourself!"*

Be careful with "get rich quick" schemes and pursue legal assistance that has tangible results. Invest wisely and expect what you have sown for your business to repay you with much more in return.

Footnote: "Go hard but be wise!"

"Be encouraged! You can fulfil your dream."
*— **Lailah Gifty Akita**ns*

#4
"Encourage Yourself"

Building a new business as a nail tech does require support, but everyone will not have this. As for me, I was fortunate enough to have my close friends and family members who allowed me to practice on them and to even sow into the business in many different ways. My support system were my first clients. They were the ones who helped spread the word about my business. Support is not always someone giving you money, but as a new nail tech, you should also view support as friends and family members, allowing you to do their nails, sending you referrals, and also sharing your new business/designs via social media.

There will be times that you may not have any support that you desire, but I encourage you to dig deep down inside to encourage yourself in those seasons.

Footnote: "Sometimes, you will have to be your own strength!!"

To keep pursuing what you have worked so hard for, you must master being your first support system. Wake up every day, knowing that you are creative, professional, and that it doesn't matter if you had one client each day or ten, that you will not abort your vision. I encourage you to speak positive affirmations over yourself daily and begin to connect with others outside of your familiar circle. Advertise and market your business like you serve thousands of clients already.

Tell yourself every day that things are going to get better if you remain focused and confident. I also encourage you to take new classes, attend nail workshops, and mingle with new technicians. Keeping your momentum must be a decision that you make daily.

Footnote: "Tough times don't last; tough people do!"

Join active social media groups for nail techs, and I also recommend that you create a blog. You will probably face a tremendous amount of competition, controversy, and criticism as a new nail technician, but when you have learned to encourage yourself and remain active within this industry, you will survive.

Your ability to survive will inspire you even the more to continue growing, serving, and building your business in excellence despite challenges. Never give up on yourself, no matter who doesn't support your business. Remember who you are when your clientele is good and when it is slow. Your love and respect for yourself and your business will determine how far you will go as a nail technician.

Footnote: "Never give up on you!"

Get up and show your face to this world daily because you play a major part is making it more exciting and beautiful in the lives of those who you serve every day.

Footnote: *"Encourage yourself, even when no one else does!"*

"Hope kept us alive in the midst of the turbulence."
— ***Lailah Gifty Akita***

#5
"Prepare For Turbulence"

As a new technician, finding a stable location can be a challenge at first. Your desire should always be to see a place that is stable, professional, and safe for your clients. You may start out renting a booth, but even if you do, please have standards and boundaries with the owner and fellow employees. The beauty salon is known as the place for gossip and jealousy, so be very careful that you are not caught up in the wind of it. Prepare to experience the possible turbulence of working in nail shops, beauty salons, &/or barbershops.

You will meet new people with all kinds of personalities, so train yourself to be respectful and cordial, but never get to close while building your brand/business.

Footnote: *"Turbulence is necessary!"*

Avoid personal relationships outside of the workplace and keep your private company to yourself. Be sure to investigate the legal status of the owner and location before signing a contract. Many shop owners hire techs and other staff and are going through eviction or foreclosure. No matter how nice it is set up, or how great the rental fee maybe, you could be walking into a trap and have to pack up and leave when things blow over.

I have worked in several shops over the past ten years, and I have seen, heard, and experienced much in doing so. I do not regret those moments, but I would like to help you so that you don't have to experience turbulence that can be avoided. Moving from shop to shop has taught me professionalism, communication, and stability.

Footnote: "Use wisdom, be professional, and always be honest!"

Always communicate about what you can and cannot do, your expectations of the owner, and make your payments on time. There will still be a little discomfort working in someone else's establishment, but until you move into your own, you must master respect and humility where you are stationed now.

Practice minding your clients and keeping a healthy workspace for them. Clients return when they are assured that they are safe and that you have their best interest. If you are forced to relocate or to expand, do so, but in modesty and respect. Never hinder the growth of your business because of personal feelings and relationships. Keep yourself in a posture to always make business moves, not personal moves.

Footnote: "Learn to adapt to changes quickly!"

Turbulence will happen, but it won't always be bad turbulence. Discern the difference and adapt accordingly. Avoid giving changes to much of your attention. You may lose passion and clients if you do not learn how to shift with whatever changes you have to make for your business quickly. Stay focused, and keep it moving!

Footnote: "Live, Lean, & Grow!"

"We know you're strong, but accepting help is its own kind of strength."
-Kiera Cass

#6
"Submit To Assistance"

It is imperative to have a mentor as a new nail tech. This will help teach you humility and train you to have a teachable spirit. Having a mentor or affiliating with another technician is very healthy if your motives are right. When you submit to assistance, you embrace countless possibilities to enhance your creativity, learn the new and old within the industry, and build your knowledge on the things that you were not taught. Having a mentor also strengthens your passion for committing, producing, and expand as a nail technician.

Witnessing the progress of someone else has the power to inspire you beyond your imagination.

Footnote: "At some point, you will need help!"

If you have the opportunity presented to you by someone integral, experienced, and happy to help you, please embrace it. Ask questions, observe, practice demonstrations you watched, and always ask can you assist in any way for hands-on training. I encourage you to seek out a mentor that can and will pour into you and not feel intimidated by you. Seek after a mentor who will not only reveal the glamour of this industry to you but who will also prepare you for the disasters that may happen in this industry.

Whatever you do, never become arrogant and feel as if you don't need help from anyone. This attitude will cause you to not only be isolated, but it may cause you to have a bad reputation for your name and business.

Footnote: "Humility will take you a long way in this industry!"

I am a pretty good nail technician, but I have never allowed myself to feel above others or to become unteachable. I knew other techs were not only better than me but that there were others who had way more experience than I did. Utilize every opportunity that you get to go online to review the work of others, watch nail care tutorials, and subscribe to YouTubers who teach in this industry for a living.

As you begin to welcome help and assistance on this new journey, always remember that you will be the one teaching and coaching others soon one day. Gather all the details, instructions, guidance, and wisdom that you can along the way to be ready to pour it all back into someone else.

Footnote: "The help that you receive may one day become the help that you will give."

It does not make you weak nor less than anyone else when you open up to receiving help. This makes you a brilliant business person who understands that support is only another step up in the industry. Learn, apply, and grow!

Footnote: "Be helped to become the help."

> *"The best way to break a bad habit is to drop it."*
> ***-Leo Aikman***

#7
"Break The Bad Habits"

As a new nail technician, you break all bad habits that may end your career before it begins. Your clientele is your bread and butter, but if they are mishandled directly or by reckless behavior, you may end up with water only. A few bad habits that you may find yourself doing is showing up late to appointments, talking or texting on your phone while working with a client, taking multiple breaks to smoke, eat or chat with fellow employees, or you may have your spouse, friend &/or family members hanging around as you work. These are all unacceptable, and if you don't plan to be organized, professional, and focused on your clients now, you will eventually gain clients and lose them at the same time. Break your bad habits before they BREAK you, literally.

Footnote: "*Bad habits can kill a good business!*"

Avoid gossiping, arguing with spouse/significant other, disrespecting fellow employees, and never talk to your clients about your personal life &/or personal issues. Practice being on time, be professional, be respectful, and eventually, you will become successful. Bad habits have been the leading cause of many business owners losing business, or even being shut down. Bad habits, whether big or small, all leave a bad taste in the mouth of those who pay you for services. You should never make your clients feel like they have to accept your bad habits, instead try your hardest to break them before they are identified and become a potential problem.

When others speak with you about your habits, never become defensive. The warning usually always comes right before destruction.

Footnote: *"Break bad habits, or they will break you."*

What you allow and do at home can't become a behavior in public, especially not in your business. Grab hold of your bad habits and seek help on how to break them and practice defeating them. Do not become comfortable with dysfunction that has the power to hinder your business from growing, being respected, or expanded further than you can imagine.

Change doesn't always feel good, but eventually, most change is for your good. If you really want to build your business, breaking bad habits must be a priority for you. You never know who will walk in to sit in your chair. You may be serving a millionaire who wants to sow into your business, and this will be determined by how you conduct yourself. Become better so that you can always go further.

Footnote: "Remain professional at all times."

"Either you run the business, or the business will run you."
— **Fritz Shoemaker**

#8
"Be Strategic"

In order to be productive, you must be very strategic. Market your business as much as you can on platforms that are available to you. Keep your business cards and appointment book on you all times. Get out into the community, malls, and local neighborhoods to pass out your flyers. Visit places that women seem to be most of the time and present your business.

Utilize social media to build and market as well to show the world that you have something that they may need. Create promotions, freebies, and shout outs to clients to make them feel appreciated and cared for. No matter how great you are, you must have a plan to gain and keep your clients.

Footnote: "Effective strategies will always lead to success."

Please also make sure that your business location is conducive for your clients. Getting clients feels impressive, but if the site is not clean, leaks are in the building, the staff is rude, and your work area is crunched or uncomfortable, you won't have them for long.

Clients expect to be relaxed, comfortable, safe, and protected from germs and bacteria. Always strive to motivate your client to desire to come again, and again. Never allow anxiousness to cause you to make decisions that may be best for you, but a dead end for your clients. Be strategic about where you decide to establish your business, how you ensure their safety, and how you will provide the best care for them uninterrupted by complaints. Most women never get a break to sit and breathe until they stop for nail care.

Footnote: "Strategizing makes room for more clientele."

It is their time to be relaxed while they beautify themselves, and your duty is to make sure they feel the peace and relaxation expected. If you have created new products, practice offering it to each client every visit, and maybe even selling it at a discounted price. If you have new products or materials being released soon, offer the pre-ordering option to your clients. Create strategies that will always keep your business fruitful and attractive. Use social on every end that you can to promote, create a following, and to advertise your work and the company.

Footnote: "Take care of your clients, and they will take care of you!"

"The key is not to prioritize what's on your schedule, but to schedule your priorities."
— **Stephen Covey**

#9
"Scheduling Matters"

Always schedule your clients, even if they are considered friends or family members. This teaches you real professionalism and how to manage your time. Scheduling should include the set time for the client to come in and start the process and time to leave open for you to break or set up for your next client. No matter what services are being rendered, I highly recommend that you schedule all clients at least 90 minutes apart. Please allow clients to schedule their next appointment upon completion, or to go online to make sure they book their slot for fills, etc.

Online scheduling is the new thing now, but I recommend that you also keep your portable hands-on scheduling book. Anything can happen via online, so it is good always to have a back-up plan to keep your business flowing

Footnote: *"Effective scheduling helps your business flow properly."*

smoothly. Scheduling is very important for you because it will allow you to see your growth, your repeated clients, and your busy/slow days. Eventually, you will be able to fix your work schedule the way you desire to have time with your family and have a personal life. Avoid overbooking!

Never schedule appointments without looking at your schedule. Use it as a cross-reference and a confirmation. Overbooking may happen once or twice in error, but please do your best to avoid it because it causes a bad look for the business and appears to be unprofessional. Your expectations for your clients to be on time and to make the required payments should match your ability to make them priority when booking.

Footnote: "Build a relationship with your scheduling book, it will help you avoid overbooking."

Practice calling clients at least two days before their appointments as a courtesy reminder and always let them know how excited you are to work with them again.

Booking will always play a critical part of your business. Although it may seem to be the easiest part, it is one of the biggest tasks to complete and should be done in excellence. Choose a booking strategy that will work for you and perfect it. Utilize your system to build your business and to be available for your clients at the time that is best for them. Book with boldness; book in excellence.

Footnote: "When you book in excellence, you serve in excellence!"

"Businesses often forget about the culture, and ultimately, they suffer for it because you can't deliver good service from unhappy employees."
-Tony Hsieh

#10
"Refresh Your Clients"

As you build your business in this industry, never forget that many others are as well. You will not only have to keep up with new designs, materials, etc., you will also have to make sure that your clients are relaxed and refreshed if needed. I suggest that you always keep small cans of juice, water, snack bars, chips &/or fruit. Most clients live hectic lives and are coming straight from work, rushing over from school, or has simply forgotten to grab a bite to eat. Always make them feel at home and that you care.

I recommend keeping a small bowl of candy, lollipops, or peppermints out as well. Clients love to experience comfort and care, so serving refreshments will allow them to enjoy while receiving your services.

Footnote: "Snacks will always bring them back!"

Other techs may not do this, but be different, be caring, and be considerate of those who keep your business open. Provide beautiful, clean serving trays.

Keep all the drinks cool and easy to access.

Always ask clients to choose from multiple options so that they feel more comfortable selecting drinks and snacks that they enjoy. It is inexpensive to keep snacks and drinks for your clients, but please be sure to manage what you have well. Always keep an inventory of what you have purchased, used, and need to re-stock. Refrain from allowing fellow employees to indulge in your client's refreshments without replacing them, and never give out more than the permitted amounts to clients.

Footnote: "Investing for your clients is always a great investment!"

Be sure to explain to your clients that refreshments are for clients only and that you will not be able to accommodate any guest. Providing refreshments should not become a burden to you, but it should bring excitement to you as you serve your clientele.

I encourage you always to make the comfort of your clients a priority. Welcome them, refresh them, and invite them back with excitement. They will never forget how you served them upon their arrival. They will tell others about it as well.

Footnote: "Treat your client well, many of them are in need of the love and care!"

"The purpose of a business is to create a customer."
-Peter Drucker

#11
"Cancellations & Rescheduling"

As you build a relationship with your clients, always go over your cancellation fees and process from the start. No client should be unaware of this, and no client should abuse the right to cancel without some consequence. The standard that you set for your business will be the one that clients will either respect or refuse services from you. Your responsibility is never to treat your business as a doormat and allow clients to do and come as they pleased. As a new technician, set order, and be consistent with keeping order.

I recommend that clients be required to cancel at least 24 hours before their appointment to leave enough time to fill that slot if needed. Once a client has repeatedly canceled and it has become a routine, a cancellation fee should be put in place.

Footnote: "Cancellations should always turn into a rescheduled appointment!"

Clients should also be asked to reschedule their appointment after cancellation to ensure that the slot is still filled. Some clients will cancel all the time. At first, be gentle and understanding, but do not allow it to continue happening without speaking to the client to reiterate your rules or to nicely ask them to find a new nail tech.

Your business is not open because of cancellations, yet it is open because of hard work, dedication, and clients who care to be served. Never be afraid to redirect clients who are not serious about doing business with you. Never feel like you have to tolerate client abuse, neglect, or tolerate cancellations when it has been done more than you desire.

Footnote: "Give respect; demand respect!"

You are important, your business is important, and cancellations are important as well. Handle them appropriately.

Footnote: "Create an atmosphere of professionalism, love, and respect.!"

> "Nothing succeeds like the appearance of success."
> -**Christopher Lasch**

#12
"You Are What You Wear"

How you dress will always dictate how you feel, good or bad. You have the freedom to dress how you desire, but I want to encourage you to make sure that it is comfortable. Many times, we desire to be cute, sexy, or even fashionable, but we often forget to make sure that we do it in modesty, safety, and comfort. There is nothing wrong with being fly nor stylish, but please be sure to add comfort to your attire. Nail technicians can sit for long hours at a time, may have to do a bit of walking depending on where they are stationed, and if you give pedicures, you will have to sit low.

I recommend that you invest in professional scrums, business polo tops, or comfortable t-shirts and slacks that are business appropriate. I also recommend that you wear shoes that are closed without a wedge or heel.

Footnote: "Be comfortable, but make sure that you are also professional!"

The clothes and shoes that you wear will play a major part in your productivity and your patience while serving your clients. Refrain from wearing clothes and shoes that are tight or torn. Avoid wearing short skirts, shorts, &/or dresses.

No matter how hot it is, remain professional and never show up for work dressed as if you are headed to a party. Always adorn yourself nicely. Make sure that your nails are nice, your hair is neat, and that you smell clean and pleasant. Your appearance matters! I suggest that you set a dress code requirement for your clients as well.

Set standards for those that you serve, and create an atmosphere where elegance, professionalism, and respect are always shown.

Footnote: "A business with standards is worth bragging about!"

Please be advised that this will all begin with you. You must set the tone for your business. You are not only the face of your business; you are also the culture of your business. What your start will have to continue as you build.

Footnote: "What you wear will determine how you perform!"

"Breathing Excitement Into Your Life."

"TIPS FOR TECHS"

- Never ignore redness, swelling, or peeling around a client's nails. Always make a decision that will help the client, not hurt them any further.

- Make sure that you have an excellent UV/ LED to cure your gel nails correctly.

- Never leave your nails tools(bits) sitting out and clean them with barbicide.

- Do not rush your work on your clients. The plan is not to have them coming back for fills to soon.

- Always keep your work area sanitized and cleaned.

- Arrive at least 45 minutes to an hour before your first client arrives at prep, set up, and to create a conducive atmosphere.

- Never steal another's nail tech's work, period!

- Wear a mask on your face for each client's service.

- Keep track of clients who are due for fills. Never let them go too long without returning for nail care.

- Never blame your clients for issues with products/equipment.

- Always check on your clients who are sick or hospitalized.

- Be wise, be nice, be productive.

"Affirmations are our mental vitamins, providing the supplementary positive thoughts we need to balance the barrage of negative events and thoughts we experience daily."
— **Tia Walker**

"Affirmations"

Every day will not be peaches and cream on this new journey as a nail technician.

There will be many days that you will feel like walking away from this industry or feel regrets for even investing in making this far.

I have created nail technician affirmations that can be used every day as you desire.

Choose two or three to say daily before leaving your house, or when you first arrive to serve your clients.

Say them, believe them, and eventually you will become them.

I am a huge believer of "you are what you speak," so speak life, speak progress, speak positivity and speak success over yourself, your business and your clients as much as you can.

- I am successful!
- I am organized!
- I am creative!
- I am needed in this industry!
- I value my clients!
- I am a professional!
- I am respectful!
- I am helpful to other techs!
- I am teachable!
- I am knowledgeable!
- I love my craft!
- I believe in myself!
- I am not in competition with anyone!
- I am confident!
- I am stable!
- I value good business relationships!
- I manage my time well!
- I am productive!

"Acknowledgements"

I could never say thank you enough to those who helped groomed me in this industry.

I am forever grateful for the many nail techs that were not afraid to pour into and help me become the nail tech that I am today.

I appreciate every piece of knowledge, wisdom, and feedback received from you.

I want to say thank you to every client who has made this position fun, exciting, and worth enduring.

I appreciate every one of my clients, and without you, there would be no me in this particular lane.

Thank you to my husband for enduring the late nights I had to work with clients, and the many times you stepped up to take care of the children, bring me lunch, and so much more.

I love and appreciate your support.

To my beautiful children, thank you for understanding the intense seasons I endured, the late nights coming home, and the times I had even to bring you to work with me.

You all give me strength, and I am happy that you are now watching the results of my hard work.

To my purpose coach, thank you for assisting me with the manifestation of this book.

I appreciate your hard work and dedication to push, inspire, and encourage me.

"Your true success in life begins only when you make the commitment to become excellent at what you do."
—Brian Tracy

Nailed It!
(Wisdom For New Nail Technicians)